CREATING JOY AND HARMONY

VOLUME 1

Richard Noel

Creating Joy and Harmony - Volume 1
Copyright © 2022 by Richard Noel

ISBN: 978-1-7330329-2-6

Printed in the USA by 48 Hour Books (www.48HrBooks.com)

DEDICATION

This book is dedicated to my father, Cyril Anthony Noel, who passed away at age 98 on February 8th, 2022, and my mother, Martina Noel, who passed away at age 89 on March 1st, 2022. He was a very vibrant, uplifting man, who always gave advice to everyone who came across his path. She was a very calm and centered woman who gave birth to nine children, and gave of her energy tirelessly. She was quite remarkable.

One of the things that I took for granted was the advice that my father and mother frequently spoke about. I realize that these powerful messages have shaped my life, to make me the individual that I am today.

These are some of their words of wisdom:

Remember, God will not do for you what you can do for yourself.

Personality has the keys to many doors, but it is the character of the person that keeps them open.

Your mind has you up, down and where you are.

Your home is your first university. What you do at home, you are going to do on the outside.

Today's world is exploitation of the needy by the greedy.

See that your brain is engaged before you put your tongue in gear.

To be effective, you must know something of everything and everything of something.

Don't do what is good, do what is effective.

INTRODUCTION

Thank you for taking time from your busy schedule to open this book and invest in yourself. My name is Richard David Noel, and I am so grateful and thankful for this opportunity to share a major aspect of my life journey with humanity. I grew up on the twin island of Trinidad and Tobago -- home of the steel pan calypso and the limbo. One thing that was evident growing up in the Caribbean was the atmosphere. It was always full of joy and festivity.

The community was always on the eve of something great and wonderful about to happen from a cultural perspective. The word "eve" appears before every holiday, bringing forth great expectations. This is the secret to tapping into the positive expectation to live a life filled with joy and harmony. Always live on the "eve" of great expectations.

In my hometown, many people did not <u>have</u> the best of everything, but they <u>made</u> the best of everything. They were able to do this by transferring their limitation of material possessions into creating the invaluable expressions of joy and harmony. That is how this book and my workshop came to be.

As a child, I was always fascinated with the festivity of the people and the beautiful cultural rhythm that surrounded me. People came from all around the globe to experience that energy and to create joy and harmony based on the experience that they encountered.

I relocated to Tucson, AZ, in 1998, with my family. We moved here for my career in aeronautical engineering. This was not my first time in the United States. I came here many times on vacation, but as I took residence and after a period of years, I identified within myself that I realized that I was losing my joy and harmony. Based on my current situation, I felt so frustrated with long work hours, working in a hazardous environment, and having a lack of work motivation.

Deep within the drumbeat of my heart, I knew that I had to make some amendments in my life, and conjure the mindset that would continuously create joy and harmony in my everyday life. So, I came upon this wonderful idea. I would bring the joy and harmony that I experienced growing up in the Caribbean, and use it as a tool to share with various communities and establishments for self-release and self-empowerment. And, I would do this with great energy and determination.

I was able to join forces with some of the local establishments to enrich the community where I live. This all started in 2003. Everywhere I had the opportunity to teach or perform the expressions of joy and creativity, people confirmed that the joy was contagious.

People always remember how you make them feel regardless if it's negative or positive. I'm so thankful that I am on the positive side of things. This gives me the opportunity to expand my territory as I meet the needs of various establishments and individuals. No matter the size of the class or event, I am able to impress upon each participant on a one-on-one basis sharing with them the importance of creating joy and harmony in their daily lives.

Regardless if it is conducting sessions with kids in crisis, substance abuse recovery clients, or just having fun, we can identify joy and learn how we can make it a part of our everyday lives so we can truly enjoy the journey of our lives. Let's make the rest of our lives the best of our lives!

What I put together in this book, Creating Joy and Harmony, is a lifestyle. My intention in writing this book is to give you the tools to overcome negative, self-sabotaging thoughts, feelings or emotions. I will prepare you to stop

6

outsourcing your power - so you can enjoy the precious privileges of life.

I always share this statement with people in all of my sessions, "Life is not what you make it, it is how you take it."

OVERVIEW

Live each day in such a way that you are truly maximizing your full potential and that you are bearing the fruits of your gift. Live from your true essence and not the expectation that was put on you. Focus not on retirement, but on enlightenment. As you live each day, ensure that you harmonize. Harmonious living is not being afraid of adding new adventures to your everyday life. Do everything from a state of joy, peace, and love.

Live in the now and not the how. Enjoy each moment, and know that every challenge that comes your way is a stepping stone and your last stone is the tombstone. Keep in mind that the desire is to live every day in accordance with your heart's desire and the passion that comes from within you. Go within or go without.

Happiness is a feeling, and joy is an emotion. Where your feelings go, your emotions flow. Your flow is the energy you generate based on how you see yourself. How you see yourself is how you reveal yourself. Creating joy and harmony is for the now, and not for the future. One of the best ways to manage your mood is to be mindful of your thoughts, feelings and emotions in the present moment, because your mood determines your attitude and altitude.

The key chapters of Creating Joy and Harmony are: I am yes I am, overcoming powerlessness, overcoming doubt, overcoming frustration, gratitude, overcoming fear, happiness, joy, and peace. Joy is contagious and harmony is flowing, everything comes together. Joy allows you to operate in a state of confidence. Harmony is required to apply to the various situations in life so that when we react according to the situation, results can be achieved.

Why do I seek joy and harmony in my everyday life?

• Sense of certainty and clarity.

• Count it all as joy – rather than ask "why me? ", say "try me", instead – look at life from a joyful, emotional standpoint, and results represent what is desired.

• Harmony vs. balance – Harmony allows all components in life to receive the necessary focus and attention necessary for the moment, while balance requires equity, when equity may not produce the desired results.

• You can only process one emotion at a time. We must make the decision of what it is that we really want.

• If it is my method to process the one emotion, joy is contagious and brings enlightenment in my life.

• See yourself as you wish to see yourself. Conjure up the thoughts and feelings that will allow you to become what you wish to see.

FOLLOW YOUR BLISS

I did not come here on earth just to go back to dirt or even to flirt. My true mission is to rebirth the essence, gifts, and talents implanted in my growth. I came not to accommodate but to infiltrate; not to debate but to facilitate. What I am giving you is not entertainment, it's edutainment.

I desire to make an imprint on your reality and a subsequent impact on society. My expression leads to my impression, as I do my best not to procrastinate, imitate or allow my work to obliviate. Rather, I subjectively choose to dominate using my conscious source and inherent faith.

Right here and right now, I am the root. You are the tree. Together, let's create the universal harmony that was meant to be.

I am not going to stress. I have the ability to conjure up the corresponding feeling that I want to caress. Regardless of my circumstances, I stand firm in my initiative power knowing that I am on a roll as I am. I am unfolding my true self and no one else, and so it is, YES, I AM!

TABLE OF CONTENTS

Dedication 3

Introduction 5

Overview 9

Follow Your Bliss.. 11

I AM, YES, I AM 15

Overcoming Powerlessness 25

Overcoming Doubt 35

Overcoming Frustration.. 45

Gratitude... 57

Overcoming Fear 69

Happiness and Joy 79

Energy, Frequency, and Vibration.................................... 89

Peace... 101

Conclusion.. 109

Expressions... 111

About Richard Noel... 113

I AM, YES, I AM

Acronym for I AM: Infinite Appointed Majestic

I AM, has been mentioned hundreds of times in many metaphysical and spiritual teachings that inspire us throughout the ages. I am not speaking metaphorically. Many of you boxing fans know Muhammad Ali and will remember his profound I am statement which was, "I am the greatest!"

What happened, as a result? He became the greatest! I AM is formless and be aware that what you put behind I AM, you become. It doesn't matter if your words are negative or positive. Water is formless. Whatever you pour it into, it takes the shape of the vessel. The power and the vibrational energetic frequency are not just in the words I AM, but also in the conscious awareness associated with every word you add after I AM.

Are you truly utilizing this inspiring law action that creates infinite possibilities? I include myself in that question. When the going gets tough and the tough get going, what do we do in these situations? Are we going to operate like the average person and say "OMG!" or stand firm in the consciousness of our I AM by affirming I AM, YES, I AM!

When you say YES, I AM, you are reaffirming to yourself the awareness of being. The awareness of being is the way to be what you want to be. Meaning that if I find myself being what I do not want to be, I must become aware of being what I want to be in order to be it.

Say I AM with that feeling consciousness must remember, that there are universal laws to this. You must, in order to feel it. If there is no feeling to it, there is no conscious awareness. And if you don't know, now you know. In a challenging situation

15

when you complain, you will just remain in the same pain again and again with no gain. When you act using the awareness of being, I AM, you regain possession once again, because you take control of your current emotional status.

Most of us say it is what it is. I believe it is what I make it to be. Life is not what you make it, it is how you take it. Instead of saying why me, say try me. In keeping with this changeless law, all things gravitate to that which is in tune. Likewise, all things disintegrate themselves which are out of tune.

Your I AM consciousness is not something that you turn on and turn off; it must become a lifestyle. Habitual, repetitious standard operating procedures just as how we learn the alphabet, and up to this day, it is still with us. Remember, we are transmitting a signal spirit, body, mind, and soul when we affirm I AM. If your cell phone signal is not strong enough, your connection will be very poor. This is why you must affirm I AM with respect and consciousness. Awareness makes it a lifestyle.

Let's do some self-reflection. I want you to just reflect on your I AM, and ask yourself if I am thoroughly a reflection of my I AM consciousness allowing the vibrational energetic frequency flow in me, through me, and as me, and how is it helping myself in my day-to-day life?

When you say I AM, it should always be in reference to the declaration you are speaking about yourself, within yourself, in the present moment or in the now. Do I have the correct word after my I AM that resonates with my expression that leads to my impression, and at the same time gives me ongoing prosperity that adds value to my life?

The greatest discovery in life is self-discovery. Until you find yourself, you will always be someone else moving to the beat of your own drum. Become yourself and no one else. The more you know about yourself, the more you grow and flow. That's the way to live from your essence and not your estimate. Do not chase after what you want. Attract your heart's desire by affirming I AM consistently. Do some self-reflection making sure you are the person you want to be right here and right now.

If not, you can make that shift by being mindful of your I AM statement because what you put after I AM, you become. I use this technique frequently if I am not in my desired mood, I am constantly repeating I am <u>about to be</u> what I <u>ought to be</u>. The word "about" always implies intent, action to be or to come.

Acronym for ABOUT: Acting Before Occasion Unfolded Truthfully

Add to your I AM subjectively. You must feel it, because subjective reality becomes objective reality. I am allowing you to discover within you that esoteric notion claims that the divine is to be discovered within you reflecting the exoteric reality. Align your inner belief to achieve your desired outcome. Again, please be mindful of what you put after I AM, because it will become your reality. Say I AM with respect, reverence, strong admiration and be mindful during the process by consciously focusing on the desired objective.

Make I AM your modus operandi. I AM consciousness is one of the best ways to align your mental and emotional forces with your intention. I AM has always played a major role in cause-and-effect throughout human existence. I AM is invoking positive kinetic energy. I AM is the embodiment of self-oneness. I AM is the only coherent universal language that produces results. I AM is living in harmony with your desires.

When you say I AM, you are declaring oneness with the infinite presence within you. When you say I am about to, it raises your awareness within you. When you add YES, I AM after your statement, you reassured yourself. I AM is the awareness of the present state of being and the awareness of your present state is the way to be what I want to be.

Affirm this to yourself every day subjectively: I AM vibrating with the energetic resonance frequency of health,

17

wisdom, and financial prosperity pure cosmic vitality every day in every way, YES, I AM.

I AM Meditation:

• Define your intention subjectively.

• Take your attention away from the obstacles that separate the objective, keeping your thoughts on the objective itself.

• Close your eyes and feel that you are living from the consciousness you desire.

• Dwell subjectively and psychologically, feeling states until you get complete assurance of your desired intention.

• I am an executive function that brings about a metacognitive approach in your everyday life.

I am love, YES, I AM love; I AM, YES, I AM!
I am healthy, YES, I AM healthy; I AM, YES, I AM!
I am strong, YES, I AM strong; I AM, YES, I AM!
I am the light, YES, I AM light; I AM, YES, I AM!
I am courageous, YES, I AM courageous; I AM, YES, I AM!
I am enough, YES, I AM enough; I AM, YES, I AM!
I am safe, YES, I AM safe; I AM, YES, I AM!
I am energy, YES, I AM energy; I AM, YES, I AM!
I am resilient, YES, I AM resilient; I AM, YES, I AM!

The above meditation is a guide, by repeating it, with respect, 108 times brings about reassurance, completion, rejuvenation, and satisfaction to your well-being. One hundred eight times is said to help bring you in harmony with the vibration of the universe, representing a journey from your mental self towards your higher spiritual self.

"I am the power of self-mastery ." - Reverend Ike

Questions to ask yourself:

1. List your core attributes.

2. What is my intention behind my "I AM"?

3. List your roles in life.

4. Now add powerful adjectives in front of each role. For example: wonderful, magical, the greatest, etc.

5. List your most empowering intentions.

I AM _____
I AM _____
I AM _____

6. Think about what you are manifesting when you say each "I AM" intention.

Write Your Answers to the Questions Here:

_____

_____

_____

_____

_____

_____

_____

_____

Chapter points to be mindful of:

1. I am infinite unconditional self-awareness.

2. Say I AM with reverence and adoration.

3. I AM is the awareness of being, and the way to be what you want to be.

4. In order to align your mental and emotional forces with your intention, saying I AM is one of the best ways to do this.

5. Subjectivity becomes your reality through objectivity, therefore you must feel your I AM as you say your I AM.

OVERCOMING POWERLESSNESS

Sometimes in life, you may lose your rhythm based on your current situations. It may be a loss of a job, a loved one, a family member, an illness, a divorce, a natural disaster, or even a global pandemic. What happens when you lose your rhythm? You stop harmonizing with your greatness, your fullest potential, your true love, and lose your purpose or direction in life. This ultimately leads to losing your joy, and you are now closed in.

Acronym for JOY: Just Open Yourself

Losing your rhythm disables your growth and development, which eventually affects your overall health.

What do we do when this situation shows up in our lives? Do we complain about it or blame ourselves and others? Most of the time when you find yourself in this situation, many thoughts come to mind. Some of these thoughts can keep you in the same place, while other thoughts can give you inspiration, guidance, and hope.

Acronym for HOPE: Having Only Positive Expectations

Based on our upbringing, we may tend to consult with a close friend, seek spiritual guidance, or share what is happening in our lives through social media to search for solutions that will bring about immediate results to bring us back in a state of control. When you are in control, you are on a roll allowing your gifts and talents to unfold.

With all this in mind and no solid solution to your present-day scenario, you feel powerless and in the state of making it very difficult to create joy and harmony in your everyday lives. We live in a universe that is governed by laws. What goes up must come down. What goes around comes around. The same principle goes to the way we feel in our powerless state of being.

I want us to take this moment and go deep - real talk. As I mentioned earlier, the universe we all live in is governed by the Law of Cosmic energy. Let's break it down.

Acronym for FEEL: Fulfilling Every Expectation Lovingly

I know you may wonder what love has to do with you in this feeling of powerlessness because all state of being starts with how you are feeling. For example, happiness is a feeling, and joy is an emotion. It's your energy in motion, in the present moment. Powerlessness is a feeling, and shamefulness is your energy in motion at the present moment. You have to always remember that during the course of the day we are challenged to encounter different feelings, and this always leads to our energy, mood, and state we find ourselves in at any given moment. This is why it is best to let our grandest feeling be a feeling of love.

Acronym for LOVE: Life Only Vital Exercise

Any unwanted feeling states that we will find ourselves in powerlessness. We must do our utmost best to evolve into a state of our heart's desire. Otherwise, we keep spiraling downward into a state of lack and limitation, and this when we start to doubt ourselves. We are going to talk more in-depth about this in the next chapter.

Based on my journey in life, many things bring about the feeling of powerlessness. Inequality towards your gender and ethnicity, long-term illness, disability, fear, uncertainty, disempowering thoughts and negative emotions, insufficient funds, inability to acquire material possessions that will lift our spirits temporarily, ability to protect ourselves from dangers and lay-off from your job leaving you unable to meet your everyday demands. Whichever of these you are navigating through mentally and physically, it is a process, and to trust the process many times, we must rely on the promises and protection of other people like politicians, spiritual leaders, protective services, close friends, etc.

The promises and reliability of others are not guaranteed. Most of the time when people fail us, we tend to keep revolving in the powerless state that we are in and not evolving as we should. Based on my observation, people who are consistently victorious promise themselves that regardless of their circumstances, they shall always prevail based on the promises they make to themselves consistently.

It's not just about making a desired promise to yourself, you have to give thanks in advance as you see and feel yourself as if you are the powerful person you desire to become. Keep in mind, right action speaks louder than words by forming a habit as you perform incantation to your promises. You have invoked the process of positive flow into your life.

Below is a guide to a pledge you can use and modify as needed to navigate your situation at the moment:

I promise myself that I am NOT in agreement with lack and limitation, rather I AM in full agreement with abundance and prosperity. YES I AM.

I promise myself that I am NOT in agreement with illness and sickness, rather I choose to agree with great health and happiness. YES, I AM.

I promise myself that I am NOT in agreement with fear, but rather I choose to always be courageous. YES, I AM.

I promise myself that I am NOT in agreement with hate, bitterness, and discord, rather I choose to live in love. YES, I AM.

I promise myself that I am NOT in agreement with procrastination. I choose to set my intentions and pursue my actions. YES, I AM.

I promise myself that I agree with youthfulness, vibrancy, energy, and cosmic vitality. YES, I AM.

Acronym for PROMISE: Putting Reassurance On Myself Is Spiritual Enlightenment

Powerlessness is one of the worst states you can find yourself in because it brings about doubt in your life. As we all know, doubt takes you out! Once you are mindful of this, always apply this! The awareness of being what you want to be means always being aware of your thoughts and feelings in the present moment, making sure that it is in alignment with the fulfillment of your heart's desire for your life.

Questions to ask yourself:

1. What are some of your daily activities that bring you happiness?

2. What memories make you happy?

3. What do these memories and activities have in common?

4. During what time of day do you feel the most powerful?

5. What are some rituals or activities you could incorporate during this time?

6. Think about living in harmony with the universal law of abundance and prosperity. What does that look like?

7. Think of a mantra or activity to start your day in a positive mood.

8. What are some ways to maintain happiness during the day?

Write Your Answers to the Questions Here:

_____

_____

_____

_____

_____

_____

_____

_____

Chapter points to mindful of:

1. What you think, you become.

2. How you feel, is what you attract into your life.

3. You turn into what you tune into.

4. What you imagine, you'll create.

5. When you complain, you remain in the same pain with no gain.

OVERCOMING DOUBT

Acronym for DOUBT: Detrimental Outrageous Unsatisfying Betraying Thoughts

When we are constantly doubting ourselves, we sometimes do the same to others and everyone around us! One of the root causes is when we focus on the how in our situation, instead of the now. In this space, we sometimes tend to procrastinate. My focus always has to be on now I have to do this and not how can I do this. The power is in the now.

I have a saying, "Doubt will take you out", meaning when you are in a feeling of doubt, it will lead us to decisions based on fear, insecurity, and indecision. We are experiencing these thoughts and emotions in the present moment as our thoughts and feelings are drifting all over the place and are not grounded as you should evolve out of this detrimental state.

This is what you do when you are doubting yourself! Immediately renounce that thought. Get into a rhythmic deep breathing pattern for a few minutes. As you center yourself, begin to affirm the opposite reality to the doubtful thought that is affecting you.

For example, if the doubtful thought is fear; affirm consciously, "I am courageous, yes, I am courageous, yes, I am, YES, I AM! Do this for at least 108 times. What this will do is supplant the doubtful thoughts with a better feeling state that is going to bring rejuvenation. As you repeat your I AM statement 108 times, your conscious awareness of your objective state will come alive. The number 108 is spiritual completion.

These negative, doubtful thoughts can also be dispelled by using an instrument such as bells, gongs, chimes, and body percussion. Because of the vibratory nature of bells, gongs, and chimes, they are extremely effective forms of mental cleansing. The tones of these instruments continue to resonate far beyond the time that you can hear them. They have been known to create spontaneous meditative states, catalyze an inner journey, and bring insight and fresh perspectives to the listener as you transcend into a state, or condition, of moving beyond ordinary limitations, physical needs and realities.

Loud-sounding objects that produce a high tonal resonance like pots and pans, also apply, as these items also produce unique tones. Body percussion such as clapping of the hands, chanting specific vocals and tones such as HA, HU, and RUM, not only stimulate the nervous system, helping to disrupt the undesirable doubtful thought, but since our body contains between seventy and eighty percent water, the intention is to produce tones that will resonate with our body's entire structure.

As you apply any of these methods, make sure to be conscious of your breathing! Deep rhythmic breathing techniques slow the heartbeat, lower, or stabilize blood pressure, and lower stress.

In the past, when I started to implement these techniques, doing it was very effective, but if I find myself in a toxic environment that is triggering doubtful thoughts, the process can become exhausting. This is when I had to promise myself only to be around quality people who can support and inspire me. If the negative environment is your home or work, please do your best to create the right mental environment for optimum results. Many times, we find ourselves in a particular state but what we have to remember is that there will be an equal and opposite reaction to the state that we find ourselves in.

What goes up, must come down. What goes around comes around. And the opposite of doubt is faith.

So many times, we are told to keep the faith or have faith. Sometimes I think that I am doing something wrong, and this is why I am having issues with these doubtful thoughts. Let's break it down. I have been using and sharing these techniques in Creating Joy and Harmony sessions and during my one-on-one private sessions called WHY.

Acronym for WHY: What Holds You

I witness major mental shifts and mental clarity from a lower state of consciousness to a higher and more relaxed state, supplanting the feeling of doubt, indecision, and insecurity.

These changes don't happen overnight. It takes getting into a habit of consistency, as you do this with reverence and adoration. Discipline the negative doubtful thoughts that everything depends on you, the individual. Living in the now, and not the how, reduces the anxiety.

Acronym for NOW: No Other Way

I promise myself that I am not in agreement with self-doubt, but rather I choose to agree with self-empowerment. Yes, I have self -empowerment. I AM, YES, I AM.

Questions to ask yourself:

1. How do you feel when you are in doubt?

2. Does doubt cause you to procrastinate? Journal about a situation that would have been different if you had no doubt.

3. Why do you think you are doubting yourself? Is this from your upbringing?

4. What is causing you to have a pattern of recurring doubtful thoughts?

5. Take a moment to reflect on what your goals would be if there was no doubt of your success.

6. Journal about how someone would tell your story in the future when your utmost goals and dreams are accomplished.

7. Make a plan to dissipate doubt with deep breathing techniques.

8. How will you keep your mind on the now and not the how?

Write Your Answers to the Questions Here:

_____

_____

_____

_____

_____

_____

_____

_____

Chapter points to be mindful of:

1. Doubt will take you out.

2. Live in the now and not the how.

3. Always focus on the now and not the how.

4. Remember to be mindful of deep breathing techniques.

5. Get into the habit of practicing modalities that will disrupt the negative doubtful feelings, thoughts, and emotions.

OVERCOMING FRUSTRATION

Throughout my entire life when I encounter frustration, and I seek advice about my concern, most of the time I am told that I need to have more patience. "Rome was not built in a day", they'd say, "you want things to happen too quickly" or "why do you want to rush everything?" I stopped explaining myself when I realized people only understand from their level of perception.

Powerlessness and doubt invoke some form of frustration upon our lives! Frustration originates from feelings of uncertainty and insecurity which stems from a sense of inability to fulfill needs. If the needs of an individual are blocked, restricted, or delayed, uneasiness and frustration are more likely to occur. This always happens when you are trying to achieve something, like completing an assignment that is due soon.

You experience frustration when it seems as if other people that you know are making progress and you are not, trying to convince someone you care about to make better choices, not getting the respect you believe you deserve in your area of influence, which usually brings joy and harmony to your life and feelings of accomplishment. Feelings of being annoyed or less confident because you cannot achieve what you want, or something that makes you feel this way, can cause you to run into problems.

Frustration is an unpleasant experience when things are not working the way you want them to work, especially those who find it difficult not to blame others for their misfortune. Frustration often leads to anger, and anger leads to pain. Pain leads to regret, and regret brings about the feeling of sadness or disappointment.

The key to frustration is that it happens when you are trying to achieve something. Frustration is often related to our inability to do things. The objects you interact with could be faulty, but they can also partially be blamed on your clumsiness, ignorance, or incompetence. As long as it is not pushed too far, frustration can drive people to become more determined to solve the case, so that they are not beaten by the obstacle. Make sure to be the hammer, not the nail.

Let's be real right here, and right now. What are some of the best choices we should make when the feeling of frustration comes upon us?

1. Stop for a moment and do your best to center yourself by doing some deep rhythmic breathing exercises for about two to three minutes. Make sure to breathe through the nose due to the benefits that are brought. It brings you into a state of equanimity, mental calmness, composure, and evenness of temper, especially in a difficult situation.

2. Talking out loud to yourself fosters self-reliance by constantly affirming I AM, YES, I AM. Be mindful of what you add to I AM, YES, I AM, because what you add will likely manifest. People that talk to themselves using I AM, YES I AM, look inward and are calling on their inner spiritual guide as referred to as intuition, the Holy Spirit, God within, and source to help us analyze situations and come to conclusions that can lead you out of your frustration. They are a saying I always referred to as, go within or go without.

3. Engage in positive activities that resonate with you and serve as a coping skill for your frustration! What resonates with me are hand drumming activities, listening to happy music, laughter, hiking in the great outdoors, jumping on my mini-trampoline, meditation, and stretching exercises. Make sure what positive coping skill activities you are partaking in resonate with you to bring forth relief and comfort.

4. Depending on the challenging task that has brought about frustration, stop and take some time off. Call upon the infinite intelligence that resides within you for guidance, right action, and wisdom to overcome your frustration. Resume when you are feeling confident once again. When frustration brings about disempowering thoughts and negative emotions, applying some of these self-help techniques may help reduce your frustration.

As a former engineer, involved in aerospace modification, one of the things that always astonishes me about flight is that the Forces or Laws of Lift, Weight, Thrust, and Drag must work together for something to fly. Similarly, the Universal Laws of Thoughts, Feelings, Emotions, and Mood must work together for people to soar to their full potential.

Now, what does this have to do with my life? It just shows that one of the best ways to get yourself out of a frustrating situation is by yielding yourself to the laws of the universe. This is when we focus on the F-ing reality: Feeling, Faith, Flow, and Fulfillment.

Feeling
How you feel is what you are attracted to in your life, so when you are in a frustrating situation, the more you complain, the longer you remain in pain. One of the best things you can do in a frustrating moment is to gather yourself together by focusing on your breath to bring yourself to the present moment. When this is achieved, ask yourself what it will feel like if I am not allowing frustration to govern my current situation and life? Take a moment subjectively, and just reflect on what will it feel like if the assignment is completed, if my heart's desires are fulfilled. As you cultivate the thoughts and the feelings of the outcome of your desire, it will begin to reflect objectively.

Well, Richard, how do I cultivate the feeling I desire? Great question! Something that I observed over the years during the holiday period and historic events as we decorate, make our favorite dishes, sing songs, and meet with friends just to cultivate and ramp up the feeling based on the occasion at hand. The only reason why we do all these things to amplify our awareness, is so we can truly use the laws to resonate with the particular occasion.

This is why it is so important to Feel your way out of the state that is not serving you and into the feeling state that resonates with your desired outcome. This is when you have to Faith it till you make it out of your frustrated state.

Faith
I mentioned this word previously. I heard this word all my life growing up in a Christian home, but it always seems to me that it was so hard to achieve. You had to be at a specific spiritual dimension to be someone of Faith. Most of the time when you are seeking advice from someone, they mention to me you need more Faith or you have to keep the Faith. It just gets me more frustrated, because it always seems like additional work, something else to add to life's equation. So what I did that makes a big difference in my life, was breaking the word faith down, applying an acronym. This is what I came up with.

Acronym for FAITH: Full Assurance In The Heart

Wow, this really changed my life! When I was growing up, if people told me to have Full Assurance In The Heart, I truly believe that it may have limited the doubtful thoughts from repetitiously trying to take me out of the joyful feeling state that I desired. Once I have Full Assurance In The Heart that is based on my Feeling state, I can take control of my situation. Then things started Flowing in my life gracefully.

Flow
What do we mean when we say get into the flow of things? When you are in flow it is like surfing with the waves in the ocean, understanding the motion and dynamic of the water, and doing your best not to go against the current. I grew up in the Caribbean, surrounded by the ocean. While growing up in this

scenery, I never attempted surfing the waves. It is not because I was fearful of what would go wrong, but it was just something that didn't resonate with me!

Surfers always talk about the best ride being when you flow with the waves. Now, when it comes to everyday life, where does Flow find its place and what is Flow? Let's break this word down:

Acronym for FLOW: Fulfilling Life's Obligation Wholeheartedly

Action Plan

I have studied a lot of successful people and one of the things they all have in common is a daily routine or ritual that allows them to structure themselves and their day more effectively. The reason for this result is that consistency forms a habit that invokes repetition, keeping them in Flow.

When you are in a state of frustration, it is very difficult to establish a positive everyday flow because you are in struggle mode.

Acronym for STRUGGLE: Stop Thinking Righteous Under Gruesome General Life Encounters

Developing a daily routine or ritual will help you release yourself from your frustrated state to a centered state of well-being. Wake up before the sun rises. Make sure you hydrate your body. Be thankful for this day. Perform meditation, prayer journaling, or do some stretching exercises. Go for a walk, jog, or bike ride, and as you exercise, keep your focus on the objective and not on the obstacles that are keeping you frustrated.

As this new inspiring action becomes a habit, you will find yourself in flow with your intended objective. Flow is important in your life. Positive cash flow brings forth financial wealth.

Blood flow brings forth healthy circulation. Spiritual flow brings forth cosmic vitality that will make you grow and glow allowing your light to shine.

Fulfillment

We all are striving for some aspect of fulfillment in our life some way or the other, but during the process, we may encounter frustration along the way. One of the key states that contributes to this is the feeling of not being enough. This is when you should turn your attention to gratitude, thankfulness, or gratefulness. As mentioned before, energy flows where attention goes. Shifting your attention will help supplant the feeling of not being enough subjectively, and allowing you to feel more than enough.

So many of us believe that the more material possessions we accumulate, the more it may give us great fulfillment and satisfaction. This is a coping comfort to our frustration and dissatisfaction in our lives, but the thing is, all the material possessions will not shield us from dispelling the thoughts and feelings that bring about the emotional consciousness of frustration.

On the other hand, acquiring material possessions as an appreciating asset for your financial growth and investment is beneficial. I would highly recommend that, because I do the same. To break things down in a nutshell, fulfillment comes from accepting what is, letting go of what was, and allowing your new, inspired action to bring forth ongoing prosperity and add value to your life.

Questions to ask yourself:

1. What is the root cause of my frustration?

2. How do I feel when I'm triggered? What can I do to return to my center?

3. Is my current situation causing my frustration or is something else causing it?

4. Am I blaming others for my own frustration, or is this something I created?

5. What changes can I make or what can I do to dispel this frustration?

Write Your Answers to the Questions Here:

_____

_____

_____

_____

_____

_____

_____

Chapter points to be mindful of:

1. Frustration originates from feelings of uncertainty and insecurity.

2. When you are experiencing unpleasant feelings because things aren't working, remember to stop and center yourself and gain composure.

3. Our inability to do things often leads to frustration, be patient with yourself.

Acronym for PATIENCE: Putting Aside Triggers In Extremely Narrowing Crucial Encounters

4. Talking out loud to yourself fosters self-reliance by constantly affirming I am. YES, I AM helps tremendously.

5. Call upon the infinite intelligence that resides within you for guidance, right action, and wisdom.

Acronym for WISDOM: Walking In Solitude During Opposing Moments

GRATITUDE

Acronym for GRATITUDE: Giving Right Action To Inner Thought Unleashing Divine Enlightenment

Why is gratitude so important to adopt in our everyday lives? Gratitude helps people feel more positive emotions, relish good experiences, improve their health, deal with adversity, and build strong relationships. As a child, my parents always told me to pray before I ate my food and when I asked why, the reply was always there are a lot of people that have nothing to eat right now, so give thanks. I did it as a formality, not understanding the cosmic law that is affiliated with gratitude.

Gratitude is not only an act that invokes the Law of Cause and Effect, it brings about a mental equivalent. When you focus on gratitude, what you appreciate expands and grows. Gratitude increases your feeling of positivity and appreciation for everything in your life. Choosing gratitude and appreciation makes a big difference because what you are grateful for, you get more. That's the law.

Gratitude is also showing appreciation for the good things and opportunities that continue to manifest as we navigate through life's everyday encounters. Gratitude will give us the power to overcome the feeling of powerlessness, doubt, and frustration. One of the best ways to stay inspired is by exercising gratitude during the day. What you are grateful for, you add more.

If you are grateful for good health, you get more good health. If you are grateful for family, you get more precious time with your family. If you are grateful for the meal that you eat, you will always be satisfied. If you are grateful for the opportunities that are allowing you to fulfill your heart's desire, more doors and opportunities will open onto you.

Gratitude is a mental awareness that is very essential to adapt into your everyday life. As I mentioned earlier, being grateful and thankful bring forth a mood of satisfaction in difficult situations. As a business owner, I witnessed gratitude working in a very powerful way in my life regardless of how many sessions I facilitated for the week. I'm still grateful and appreciative for the opportunity and privilege to support the clients' emotional distress.

One very effective technique, that I normally do when I have a slow day, week, or month, is to look at my schedule and say I remember when my days, weeks, and months were slow. Now, I am in high demand for my products and services, and I am good to go! I am grateful. I'm thankful in advance!

By saying thank you in advance, it gives you that faithful assurance and appreciation that what you desire is about to objectify what you are grateful for. You add more thinking of gratitude as being privileged, which allows you to do what you want to do, have what you want to have and be who you want to be.

One of the things that we always take for granted is that life is a privilege and nothing is guaranteed. I know when we wake up every morning we say thank you, but we don't have to wake up every morning. There are so many people who did not make it. Each and every day, you have an opportunity to let your light shine, or to allow yourself to bear fruit. We always have to remember that we are privileged for the opportunity.

I've seen a new day, so my routine every day is as I wake up, I give my infinite intelligence, my God, my source (or your preference of inspiration) thanks for giving me the privilege of seeing another day! I'm so grateful and thankful in advance, so I am expecting to create a day that I am truly designing.

As I mentioned earlier on, be who you want to be, have what you want to have, and do what you want to do, because you live every day and you die once. Every day, you enjoy the privilege of being alive. Making sure that you are following your bliss and living the life that you desire. What prevents us from really focusing on the privilege of life is when we allow the emotional garbage that keeps us in bondage. This makes us think like savages.

By using different modalities that resonate with you, do your best to adapt habits that will not allow the negative emotions of fear, doubt, indecision, grief, and guilt stop you from truly enjoying the privilege of life. Remember, nothing is guaranteed. One of my favorite quotes is "Every challenge is a stepping stone, and your last stone is the tombstone". Use your set-back as a set-up for your comeback and exercise gratitude during the process.

Sometimes you may desire something for your life, and it is taking time. Everything is a process, as we all know. Most of the time, we tend to look at the things that are holding us back from achieving our heart's desire. Most of the time, this brings about frustration, blockages, and discomfort, making it seem impossible to accomplish the things that we are desiring.

We tend to complain about our situation, and when you complain, you remain in the same pain, with no gain. As you shift your focus to gratitude, I've seen being grateful and thankful for your current situation bring a sense of calmness and trust. Focus towards your desired outcome and faith it till you make it.

A couple of years ago I started to practice a gratitude ritual, which just takes a couple of minutes to perform. While I'm lying in bed, I place my right hand on my heart and I focus on three things that I am grateful and thankful for.

When I'm in a Theta brain wave state, meaning before I fall asleep, or when I'm about to wake up, I give thanks in advance for a wonderful day. A critical part of gratitude is having consistent faith. Even when you don't know what the outcome is going to be, you must have the confidence that it will all work out. When you are dealing with undesired circumstances, have gratitude for them as well.

1. I am so grateful and thankful for the privilege of waking up to this beautiful day.

2. I am so grateful and thankful in advance for the outcome of this beautiful day. Life is good.

3. I am about to become one of the best versions of myself today.

4. This is the day that the divine one has made, let me rejoice and be glad in it.

Use this as a guide for creating the world you desire. Furthermore, we have seen that when we become aware that a benefit might not exist, we tend to become more appreciative and grateful for that benefit. Good health, even if your health isn't great. It could be worse, and you likely still have some working parts to be thankful for.

Ways to show gratitude:

Put your gratitude on paper. Write down the names of three people or things in your life you are grateful for.

Having a gratitude conversation frequently with friends and family members can have a positive effect on our friends and family, too.

Tell someone you appreciate them. Pay it forward.

It is often stated, "During difficult times, gratitude is more important than ever". Research shows that gratitude can help us cope with traumatic events, regulate our negative emotions, and improve our well-being. More importantly, it's a small way to have a meaningful impact.

Being grateful is always telling yourself, I am thankful for this moment despite what I am going through, waiting on, or expecting to transpire in my life. I am thankful, YES, I AM. By affirming consistently what you are grateful for, each day, you will develop an inspiring action that will bring forth peace in your life. A good practice is to pause when you find yourself unhappy with someone or something, use the 17-second rule by pausing, focusing on your breath, allowing yourself to get to a state of equanimity, mental calmness, and composure in a difficult times. Visualize, with as much intensity as possible, the strong, positive emotion associated with achieving your ultimate vision by focusing only on the objective. Declining obstacles holding these thoughts and feelings in your mind will begin their transition from a negative state toward an uplifted state of gratitude and appreciation.

Questions to ask yourself:

For the next week, journal what you are grateful for.

1. Why is it important to be grateful regardless of circumstance?

2. Am I only grateful when I receive what I want or can I also be grateful when things don't go my way?

3. How can I incorporate being thankful as a lifestyle and practice, rather than a one time thing?

4. When I make being grateful a daily practice, what do I notice about how I feel?

5. As I am feeling lack, jealousy, or inadequacy, how can I shift to a mood of gratitude?

Write Your Answers to the Questions Here:

_____

_____

_____

_____

_____

_____

_____

_____

Chapter points to be mindful of:

1. Always be grateful in advance.

2. What you are grateful for, you add more.

3. Contentment isn't an exciting kind of happiness. It's more like peaceful ease of mind.

4. Being grateful always is telling yourself I am thankful at this moment despite what I am going through.

5. Gratitude is an emotional state of satisfaction that can be seen as a mood mental state.

OVERCOMING FEAR

Acronym for FEAR: Fuck Everything And Rise

Fear is one of the most self-destructive feelings you can find yourself with:

Fear of losing a loved one
Fear of ill health
Fear of old age
Fear of losing your valuable possessions
Fear of death
Fear of rejection
Fear of the unknown

Based on your thoughts, what is coming to you is coming from you. What is coming from you is coming right back at you. The fear is in the thought, and the thought is in the fear. The cause is in the effect and the effect is in the cause.

Always be mindful of your attention; it will determine your ascension and descension. There are two types of fear: moderate and extreme. Moderate fear is like the first time experiencing a new job, moving to another state or county, engaging in a new activity, driving to a new location on your GPS and it loses its signal! Extreme fear on the other hand is a negative emotion that you consistently and continually ruminate on, like losing valuable possessions, self-rejection, self-doubt, dissatisfaction, fear of the unknown, and fear of a bad outcome or bad news.

The opposite of fear is courage. It's best to confront your fearful thoughts and feelings because on the other side of fear is glory. What this means is, if you truly face your fear, there is victory and glory on the other side of that fear. I am certain at some time in your life you have experienced when you overcame something you were fearful about. Afterwards, you automatically conjure up the courage and strength to face it again. The more you do it, the better you get. The better you get, the more you keep doing it. So keep doing it.

Keep facing your fears. I had some very fearful experiences in my life. When I look back at all the scenarios, I'm so grateful and thankful because of my boldness and courage to add value to my life. I end up experiencing victory and glory. One of the most fearful moments of my life is when I had a home invasion at my residence. Even though a gun was pointed to my head, for some reason I knew that I would come out of this alive. I will never forget; things happened so quickly in this moment. I was telling myself it's going to be OK. Regardless of the outcome, I will be victorious and end up on the side of glory.

I have mentioned glory several times. Here is what I mean by that. The definition I like when referring to glory is: something that is regarded with such splendor that it is so overwhelming and quite powerful. Because of this thought process, you overcome your fears. The reward on the other side of fear is glory. Fear is the currency of control, what you fear comes upon you. Energy flows where attention goes.

One of the ways to get negative behaviors to change is to identify the subconscious habits based on fearful thoughts, and what triggers them. You can do this through releasing, forgiving and flooding your subconscious mind repeatedly with the opposite reality so it will crowd out the negative and fearful thoughts. What we have to acknowledge is extreme fear turns into phobia. The reason you need to manage your fear and not allow it to manifest into phobia is because you cannot function effectively. The definition of phobia is an extreme or irrational fear of or aversion to something. Many times, the fearful thoughts we think don't come to pass.

Acronym for PHOBIA: Pararalyzing Horrifying Occurrences Bringing Internal Anxiety

You turn into what you tune into. The takeaway here is to rise up from fear.

This means fear is something that shows up in your thought pattern, and you need to incorporate modalities in the opposite reality, which is courage. The definition of courage is: the ability to do something that frightens one. On the other side of fear is victory and glory!

Questions to ask yourself:

1. How often am I thinking fearful thoughts?

2. Are the things that I am fearful about manifesting in my life?

3. What am I tuning into that is bringing these fears upon me?

4. What are the fearful scenarios in my life that are turning into phobias?

5. How can I focus more on courage and facing my fears?

Write Your Answers to the Questions Here:

Chapter points to be mindful of:

1. When you are feeling that you are <u>not</u> in control, you are in an energy state of fear. An example of this is watching the news. Typically, the news covers stories that are attention-grabbing. The saying for a good news story is, "If it bleeds, it leads."

2. Be mindful of where your attention is focused. It will determine your direction, either to be ascending or descending.

3. Think of a time when you were in a stressful and fearful situation and you were calm. This is an example of not thinking fearful thoughts. You already knew the outcome would be glorious. Rinse and repeat.

4. Remember to consistently affirm courage to the subconscious mind, and it will replace the fear and insecurity of the unknown.

5. You become what you think about, and what you think about you bring about. Don't allow fear to mess up your career.

HAPPINESS AND JOY

This is one of my favorite chapters - happiness and joy. I often wonder why I'm so fascinated with this feeling. It goes all the way back to my childhood. I grew up on the twin island of Trinidad and Tobago, where the people in the islands did not have the best of everything, but they made the best of everything. I could vividly recall the joy and essence based on our heritage and cultural practices that constantly invoked happiness, at the same time bringing forward true joy to our communities.

I realized after a while, when I had come to the United States to work in aeronautical engineering, that I had lost this happiness and joy from my childhood. I felt stuck. This was a pivotal moment for me, because I knew I had to create a new path for myself here in the United States. What excited me about this realization is the prospect of knowing that I could turn a very painful moment of being stuck into a career that didn't invoke this joy. It could become something based on the culture that I came from.

Many of us find ourselves in jobs or careers that don't fit with who we are or what gives us joy. The trick is to tap into what makes you happy and focus on what brings you joy. You can do this by recalling happy memories from your childhood. How you think is what you become.

Happiness is a feeling, and joy is an emotion. I did not have to reinvent the wheel based on my upbringing and from what I have experienced on a daily basis. I created programs, and I offer them to the community to conjure up happiness and joy. What I love most about this journey is that people embrace what I have to offer, and to this day I have not looked back.

The reason I tell you this story is because if you are seeking happiness and joy in your everyday life, you must create it. Each year, there are various holidays that the cultures celebrate. Keep in mind that for each and every holiday, there is a feeling that comes with the holiday. This is created by using different decorations, themes, songs, scents, moods, and feelings. This ritual of celebrating the holidays sets the tone.

Let's dive deep into this narrative. If you want to create the feeling of happiness and joy in your life, you have to focus on your thoughts. Happiness is a feeling; joy is an emotion. Emotion is energy in motion. The more you conjure happiness, you continue to stay in the mood of emotional joy.

There's a statement every day that I always mention - you live every day and you die once. Life has its challenges. Each and every one of us has to navigate life's challenges with the tools we have. I also refer to this statement - life is not what you make it, but how you take it. How you take life is how you are responding when things come before you that steal your happiness and your joy.

Now, I know in everyday life, there are things that will definitely bring you down. Maybe you may hear some difficult news via a text or an email, or a story about a family member or friend. Our loved ones can evoke emotions of sadness, anger, or disappointment. These things do happen, but they should not be our resting place. Allow yourself to feel those emotions, but let them move through you.

Your intention should always be to get to that higher place within yourself that will invoke that feeling of happiness and bring forth the emotion of joy. It is contagious. As we know, meeting your joyful presence will liberate others who need joy. What is coming to you is coming from you, and what is coming from you is coming right back at you. Happiness is your birthright; joy is your way of life. Joy is not just relegated to the holidays.

CREATING JOY AND HARMONY

We all like to be around people who are pleasant. Their mood comes from their thoughts and emotions. If at the present moment you are not in the mood that you are desiring, what are you thinking about? What are you feeling? What is the emotion that is bringing about that undesirable mood? If you want to change your current mood, you have to change your thoughts that bring about the feeling and the emotion of your desirable outcome.

Let's start from the top. Regarding this cosmic energy flow, how you think you become, and you become what you think about. How you feel, you attract into your life. Where your feelings go, your emotion follows, which leads you to your resting place that we call mood. When you are trying to solve a problem, pay attention more to how you feel and less on what to do. Feel your way through it. You turn into what you tune into.

The manifestation process begins once a single thought has been held for 17 seconds. It has been proven that if a negative thought remains longer than 17 seconds, it takes residence within the mind. If you allow a negative thought to remain for longer than 17 seconds - the rumination process begins. This is a tendency to repetitively think about the causes, situation, and consequences of a negative emotional experience.

Here are a few strategies to try that will stop the effects of ruminative thinking:

• Positively distract yourself by engaging in pleasant activities such as exercise or hanging out with friends.

• Stop that train of thought.

• Write it down.

• Meditate.

Meditation is medication for your spiritual sensation. This is why it's important to be mindful of your thoughts and feelings. When you find yourself in the 17 second rule, stop the transmission and tune into an uplifting state. Keep the focus on a positive outcome rather than feed into the negative feelings. These are low vibrations and they disrupt the frequency of positive feelings.

Your thoughts create your electrical impulses, and your feelings are your magnetic waves. As these two form a union, be mindful of your intentions. Only resonate with the thoughts and feelings that serve your highest purpose. Your emotion is energy in motion that is generated by your feelings, and your mood is your anchored resting state. This is why it's very important to be mindful of how you fall asleep and the state of being in which you fall asleep. I recommend that before you go to bed, always put yourself in the frame of mind that, "on the eve of", something great is coming your way.

Just as you would think on Christmas Eve and New Year's Eve, you anticipate great and joyous feelings. You are conditioning the subconscious mind that controls 95% of your life. As you are in a state of rest, your subconscious mind is still in motion. Meaning, as you fall asleep, if you are thinking about lack, limitation, guilt. fear, doubt, or indecision, that is what your thoughts are going to create in the coming day.

You can stop those negative, downward spiraling emotions by thinking, feeling, and speaking things of a more positive nature, the outcomes that you would like to manifest in the upcoming day. The word "eve" is not just a reference for Christmas or New Year's Eve. It is always in reference to happy and joyful expectations and anticipation in regards to the upcoming day.

Questions to ask yourself:

1. Am I following my bliss?

2. What am I looking forward to each day?

3. Where in my life am I waiting on permission to create joy or be happy?

4. When have you realized that something you were doing for a living, either a job or career, wasn't in alignment with who you are or what you know?

5. If I notice that something is stealing my joy or happiness, what thoughts can I think to create the feeling or mood that will have a desirable outcome?

Write Your Answers to the Questions Here:

Chapter points to be mindful of:

1. Happiness is a feeling. Joy is an emotion.

2. Where your feelings go, your emotion follows. Emotion is energy in motion.

3. Hold a positive thought for 17 seconds, several times during the day. This will enact the vibration for manifesting what you want to attract.

4. Do what positively inspires you and makes you come alive.

5. Even though something disappointing happens, count it all as joy.

ENERGY, FREQUENCY, AND VIBRATION

Acronym for ENERGY: Engaging Natural, Emotional Reaction Generated Yourself

"We live in a universe that is governed by laws, and as individuals, for us to truly resonate harmoniously with these laws, we need to think in terms of energy, frequency, and vibration" - Nikola Tesla

What goes up must come down. What goes around comes around. What you put out into the universe comes right back at you. The law of cause and effect or the boomerang effect, how does this apply to us in our everyday lives?

<u>What is Energy?</u>
It's the foundation of your emotion based on what you generate off of your thoughts and feelings. It cannot be destroyed. Be mindful of your energy, because it creates your synergy. We are given two currencies every day, energy and time.

Acronym for TIME: Tapping Into My Energy

It's your set point of energy. Where and what are you plugged into? An example of this is when you go to a coffee shop and search for a Wi-Fi connection. Frequency is coming from that Wi-Fi signal. If you yawn, a frequency is created. It's contagious. When you see someone yawn, you typically yawn. Frequency travels in a spiral, not linearly. Upward generates positive and downward generates negative.

Everything is Energy, and that is all there is to it. Match the frequency of the reality you want, and you cannot help but get that reality. It can be no other way. This is not philosophy.

ENERGY GATES

- Crown Energy Gate- Blocked By Ego Attachment
- Third Eye Energy Gate- Blocked By Illusion
- Throat Energy Gate- Blocked By Dishonesty
- Heart Energy Gate - Blocked By Grief
- Solar Plexus Energy Gate- Blocked By Shame
- Sacral Energy Gate- Blocked By Guilt
- Root Energy Gate - Blocked By fear

<u>What is Frequency?</u>

It's a feeling. It's your set point of energy - where and what you are plugged into. It's kind of like tuning into a radio station. You have to be tuning into the music you want to listen to just like you have to be tuned into the energy you want to manifest into your life. Frequency travels in a spiral, not linearly. Upward, generates positive feelings, and downward generates negative feelings. If you are vibrating in the frequency of love, joy and abundance, you are going to attract things that support that frequency.

The universe responds to your frequency. It doesn't recognize your personal desires, wants or needs. It only understands the frequency in which you are vibrating. For example, if you are vibrating in the frequency of fear, guilt or shame, you are going to attract things of a similar vibration. Change your mindset, it will change your life.

EVOLVING

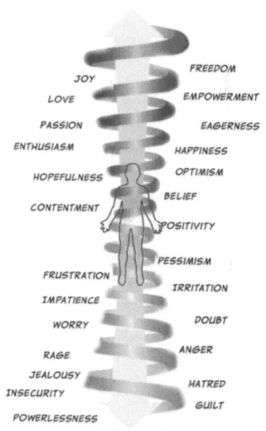

JOY
FREEDOM
LOVE
EMPOWERMENT
PASSION
EAGERNESS
ENTHUSIASM
HAPPINESS
HOPEFULNESS
OPTIMISM
CONTENTMENT
BELIEF
POSITIVITY
PESSIMISM
FRUSTRATION
IRRITATION
IMPATIENCE
WORRY
DOUBT
RAGE
ANGER
JEALOUSY
INSECURITY
HATRED
GUILT
POWERLESSNESS

REVOLVING

What is Vibration?

Vibration, or Universal Life Energy, is simply a method to describe your overall state of wellbeing. Everything in the universe is made up of energy vibrating at different frequencies. Even solid objects are made up of irrational energy fields, including you. Vibrations operate at high and low frequencies. This is true for the vibrations that occur within our beings, too.

Lower vibrations of being are associated with disempowering thoughts, negative emotions, poor health and lack of spiritual awareness. Higher vibrations, on the other hand, are associated with empowering thoughts, positive emotions, good health and strong spiritual awareness.

For example, look at your Wi-Fi signal. In your residence, you have a strong signal, vibrating high. When there is interference in the signal, it gets weak, vibrating low. The signal revolves high and low, and we do the same. We keep revolving and not solving anything in life, instead of evolving when the signal is weak.

Ways to raise your vibration:

• Good health.

• Think positive emotions.

• Thinking empowering thoughts.

• Self-awareness and mastery.

• Go where you are celebrated, not tolerated.

• Go where you feel adored, not where you feel ignored.

• Go where you feel happy, not where you feel crappy.

• Go where you feel loved, not where you feel shoved.

• Go where you feel like a king, not like a ding-a-ling.

• Go where you feel like a goddess, not where you feel modest.

Questions to ask yourself:

1. Am I in my true place and doing what I want?

2. What will happen if I apply these concepts to my life?

3. Is my energy contagious or outrageous?

4. If my current situation isn't desirable and is somehow related to my lack of awareness, how can I change my frequency and vibration to create a positive outcome?

5. In order to generate positive energy, what can I do?

Write Your Answers to the Questions Here:

Chapter points to be mindful of:

1. Look for ways to raise your vibration.

2. Raise your vibration for good health.

3. Energy flows where attention goes.

4. Positive energy is something you generate.

5. Frequency is an energetic set point. What you are plugged into, you get sucked into.

PEACE

Acronym for PEACE: Pursue Excellence And Cherish Everyone

I love this acronym I came up with for peace. It gives me more meaning and understanding towards the world. The only justice in life is just as you think. As a mind thinks, so it is. It's important for us all to live in peace. I grew up in the Catholic religion. One of the things the priest instructed us to do after the service was to repeat, after him, a profound statement:

Priest: Peace be with you
Congregation: And also with you

At that stage in my life, I did not grasp the profoundness of that statement. Anytime I hear the word peace, I always think of peace in the world. However, the purpose this really served was to create peace within myself, which would then radiate out into the world. Peace begins with you.

During my journey, I have seen so many organizations, groups and activists show their passion for peace, but it is more of a reaction of how they feel towards the lack of peace. For example, in the occasion when there is an incident against humanity in our communities that evokes anger and outrage. At that moment, it appears there isn't a solution in sight but to act violently by making choices that we regret.

You can be concerned, but not be consumed. When you are consumed, it affects your vibrational frequency and makes you unstable. This creates a loss of peace. Not only in your mind, but in your soul. When you are in a calm state of mind that feels peaceful, make your decisions from this frequency and vibrational set point. When we are in a Beta brain wave pattern, (anxiety and fight or flight), we lose blood flow to the forebrain, which challenges the decision-making process. When we are in a Theta brain wave pattern, (rest and digest), we are relaxed and in a meditative state of mind. The forebrain governs 40 percent of our problem-solving and decision-making skills.

Corrupt communication steals your peace. Be mindful of what you watch and listen to. Dealing with OQP, Only Quality People, equals positive connection and not rejection, because connections have no complexion. Be aware of your self perception. If you are feeling inadequate, this will affect how you live your life and communicate with others. You will not have peace. Live from peace. Allow yourself to enjoy the privileges of life.

Acronym for PRIVILEGE: Precious Rights Invoking Various Inspiring Life Entitlement Granted Emotions

Make decisions where your future self will thank your present self, because what you are thinking and feeling right now has a positive or negative effect on your future. Your future is in reference to what you are thinking in the present moment.

Life is a privilege. Make a promise to yourself not to allow the emotional garbage to keep you in bondage and have you thinking like a savage. Peace be with you.

Questions to ask yourself:

1. How do I feel when I am at peace?

2. What can I do to create peace of mind?

3. When I'm in a difficult situation, what peaceful thoughts can I think?

4. Where in my life can I make decisions from a place of peace?

5. Who am I when I am peaceful?

Write Your Answers to the Questions Here:

Chapter points to be mindful of:

1. Peace begins with you.

2. I need to be aware of my self-perception to create peace.

3. Make decisions where your future self will thank your present self.

4. The only justice in life is just as you think.

5. Bloom where you are planted. Peace is within you.

CONCLUSION

I want to remind you as you finish this book to stop outsourcing your power to others. Seek self-mastery. This means, be aware of your power within and realize that you always have it. Do what you need to do, be who you are meant to be, and be mindful of your thoughts, feelings, emotions and moods.

Creating Joy & Harmony is a lifestyle - it's meant to be lived, not just read. Each of the chapters are designed as reference tools - refer to them often, as you would refer to a GPS giving you turn-by-turn directions to get to your desired destination.

Nourish your mind daily and intoxicate your feelings with loving, positive and effective ideas. Life is short. Stop putting off things for later. Go on that trip now. Ask that person out. Make that move to a different place. The concepts I've shared with you in this book are meant for the now - not yesterday or later.

My intention in writing this book is to give you the tools to overcome negative, self-sabotaging thoughts, feelings and emotions so you can enjoy the precious privileges of life. Remember, abundance is your birthright, and prosperity is your way of life.

Take care of yourself first, otherwise you'll end up in a hearse!

EXPRESSIONS

When you are conscious of your mood, it brings about self-mastery, a collective objective that gives you a mindful perspective, allowing you to be positively connected and receptive.

It is good to love the life you live and live the life you love. Find a way to give, expect the best, and continuously find ways to release and eradicate emotional stress.

Go where you are adored, and not where you are ignored.

When you have a problem, it's not really about what to do. It's about how to feel, because how you feel is what you'll attract.

Surrender to what is, and let go of what was. Allow your new and inspiring actions to create ongoing prosperity in your life.

What gets you there will not keep you there. Renew your mind every day.

If you are not loving the life you live, remember, life is a privilege. Don't let the emotional baggage keep you in bondage and have you thinking like a savage.

Your present mood brings about the revealing attitude that reflects your personality, manifesting your future reality in our environmental society.

Do your best to form a habit of conjuring up positive moods and enhancing activities such as listening to your favorite music, being mindful, journaling, connecting with nature, and sun exposure.

What you fear, will appear. What you hate, you stimulate. What you fight, will ignite. What you resist, will persist. This is why you have to take the risk to follow your bliss.

When you're feeling down, and being happy is hard, stand by the mirror and pretend to be glad. Try to smile and muster a grin. Then think to yourself, "I'm going to win!" When situations are grim, and the pressure is on, don't be discouraged by others who look at you with scorn. Get on with this precious life. Muster a grin. Think to yourself, "I'm going to win!" Many a man and woman have gone down failure's avenue, but gathering courage, they fought on in hope. Don't give up here on life's slippery slopes. Strive to be strong and never quit. When failure seems near, get the fighting spirit. Get on with life, and muster that grin. Think to yourself, "I'm going to win!"

ABOUT RICHARD NOEL

Richard Noel facilitates Creating Joy and Harmony workshops for large groups, as well as private individual sessions that focus on sound therapy. His objective in leading these workshops and private sessions is to release people from negative emotional distress. He has spent the last 20 years of his lifetime using percussion as a positive modality to influence people through delivering a rhythmic experience they will never forget. Richard also helps facilitate various local festivals.

He encourages community reconciliation through annual events such as "Drum Up For Peace," in collaboration with "International Day of Peace." His heartfelt dedication to his practice inspires his keen intuition as he applies rhythmic tones, vibrational frequencies and incantation techniques to guide individuals along a healing journey and reconnect with their authentic selves.

Richard is an author, producer, and keynote speaker. He is the CEO of Jam2Grow. You can read more about Richard and the wonderful work he does with people, as well as read letters of recommendation from various civic and governmental agencies he's worked with, and individual testimonials from people who have benefitted from his work. These can be found on his website: www.Jam2Grow.com